ABOUT THE AUTHOR

Nikos Savvakis was born in Finikounda, a small fishing village in the South-Western Peloponnese, Greece. He attended high school in Kalamata, the nearest big town, and attended university in England, reading Politics. He has published five collections of poetry.

DEDICATION

To my friend Kenneth Badger

Nikos Savvakis

TAKH
The Spirit

AUSTIN MACAULEY PUBLISHERS™

LONDON • CAMBRIDGE • NEW YORK • SHARJAH

A CIP catalogue record for this title is available from the British Library.

ISBN 9781398410855 (Paperback)
ISBN 9781398410862 (ePub e-book)

www.austinmacauley.com

First Published (2021)
Austin Macauley Publishers Ltd
25 Canada Square
Canary Wharf
London
E14 5LQ

I have always loved animals. My constant encounters with both domesticated and wild, as a boy in a village, impressed me for life. In our stable, next to the house, a tiny she-donkey and a young horse were members of our family.

In the 'exile' of my summer holidays to a nearby mountainous village, I would live a daily 'miracle'. Every day, at dusk, a herd of goats would pass outside my grandparents' home. On hearing the bells of their approach I would climb on the wall of the courtyard and, enchanted, would absorb the sight, the sound and the smell of the colourful crowd.

Another wonderful spectacle was the animals of the gypsies. It must have been a matter of pride and prestige amongst them to have their horses and donkeys as beautifully decorated as possible.

Some of my friends, armed with slings, would hunt little birds, especially at night with the help of a torch, on the trees where they were sleeping.

I never had a sling or joined them in their expeditions.

NIKOS SAVVAKIS

POEMS

The Descendant of Amalthea

A pulsating colourful carpet
Constantly changes patterns and dimensions
As it is climbing the slope of the mountain.

Its minimalist music
Matches perfectly
The meditation halls
Of the New Age freaks.

Jean-Baptiste Grenouille bypassed
The musk of the leader of the herd.
The laboratories of Eau de Cologne

Placed it imperatively
In the *nécessaire* of the male.

Even though it preceded
Many of the domesticated
It did not adorn the "gallery" of Lascaux.

Perhaps because even today
Her own *modus vivendi*
With *homo sapiens* remains unfulfilled.

Chloi Amolindi "Pure Flora" could perfectly be
The scientific definition of her food.

The grass Her Highness
Is prepared to consider proper for consumption

Must meet absolutely
Her own very demanding criteria.

Her fundamentalism
In eclectic nourishment

May result in her being banished
From civilisation.

The steppes of Mongolia
And the inaccessible slopes
Of Asia and the Andes

May in the near future
Become her unique habitat.

In gastronomic popularity
It may deservingly stand next to
The fin of shark.

The margin is by definition
The harbour of
The unadoptable.

Despite Being a Few

If not the number one idler in Nature
It is with great difficulty
That one will come across
A second contender of the title
With such an impaired *curriculum vitae*
In abandon and *a cappella* opera.

The eternal food-gatherers
Having won over *Homo sapiens*
In his agricultural stage
They succeeded in baptising
– This unrepentant devotee of *bel canto* –
Useless by definition.

Considering singing for the pure pleasure
Of the activity in itself
Meaningless,
– It does not spring from joy, sadness, enthusiasm
Madness, etc. – they bestowed on the interpreter
The title of professional idler.

However some – admittedly few
But existent – farmers in Thrace
Along with the baking of the first bread
They make the cicada-bread-roll
The share of the tireless bard
Who tempers their fatigue
With his exquisite gift.

Urban Encounters

The crossing of Avenue Amalias
In front of the "Great Britain" hotel is tantamount to Russian roulette
In its Greek version;
In other words, defective.

The stray-dog waited patiently
Next to me at the traffic-lights.
I prompted him and we crossed together
To the median.

At our second exodus
He followed two metres behind me.

At the third and last crossing
I was hesitant;
Yes, the light was green, we could cross
But the taxis formed a parading convoy.

My fellow-traveller, cool-headed,
Led the way;
Hesitantly and on alert
I become his tail.

On reaching the square
He turned left
To kill time at his usual spot
And I straight towards the "Winds"
For my "morning prayer",
The reading of my newspaper.

All wishes
Are to be respected
In co-existence.

Stray-Dogs in Squabble

The pack walked exhausted and bloody,
The night had been exceptional,
Memorable one could say.

The thirst had been quenched,
The hunger satisfied,
The fury appeased.

The lust alas,
A ceaseless fire
Burning their entrails,
Remained.

Lament of Alecos

A "jump" from the village
"Megala Alonea".
In the summer
They were a furnace at 42°C
With a baked country road.

Inaccessible with the coming
Of Autumn
As the sky emptied
Its skinbags

And the absolute
Dominion of mud

Made the crossing
Of the jungle

A piece of cake
By comparison.

The "battle" of olive-gathering
Was a constant
Guerrilla warfare
Between rain and clear skies

Without the luxury
Of a short ceasefire.

People and animals
Were soaked to the bone
In sweat and rain.

The wet sacks
Made the weight
Too heavy to lift.

In vain did the animals try
To find a dry piece of road to step on
And not be plunged into mud up to the knee.

The torture of transport
Could not be borne by all.

The weak legs of the tiny she-ass
Did not stand the heavy weight,
One broke.

She was unloaded
And dragged to the bank
Of the nearby river.

In the evening
And during the "flood"
It was impossible to find a rifle.

The next day Alecos,
The young stallion and her company,
Was looking for her
Whinnying restlessly

While her body
Was "sailing" far off the shore.

Takh – The Spirit

Whistlejacket had the honour
He deserved and was painted by the brush
Of the admirer of the species *par excellence,*
George Stubbs.

Four of his forebears
Since they left the hands of Lysipos
And wandered for a while
Today they adorn the Basilica
Of St Mark in Venice.

The homage to the descendants of Voucephalas
Renders unto Caesar his due.

The father of the Macedonian
Celebrated his victory at the race in Olympia
More than the birth of his son
At the same day.

Delighted to the same extent
Are the Mongols too
Who enjoyed Buzkashi long before?
They included polo in their athletic repertoire.

The intervention of the Pope
Was essential in order to cease being consumed.
Feeding is his constant worry
Since it has almost done away with sleep.

The "avenues" to his heart
– As every groom knows –
Are chatting and scrubbing.

The Cossacks, his generous friends,
Dispose, only for the shades of red,
62 words. Their wives
Would be more than delighted with one third, for themselves.

Their empire,
Like all the others,
Including that of the Stars and Stripes,
Was based on the saddle.

The toga and the sandals
Of the Eternal City
Were the result of the horror
Of the patricians

Vis-à-vis the barbarian centaurs
In trousers
And boots.

The Apaches and the Comanches
Sent the Spaniards for re-examination
In riding horsemanship
After the great present of the Old World to the New.

John Wayne and Pancho Villa
Owe their existence
To the 24 studs and 10 mares
That Christopher brought in his second voyage.

Zad el-Raheb
"The Gift of the Rider" was a present of King Solomon
To the Arabs!

Gallant at his wedding
To the Queen of Sheba
He donated to the subsequent
Devotees of the Prophet

The founder of the most thoroughbred
Branch in the world.

The love of Philip Astley for the species
Founded the circus,
With the exact opposite outcome
Of the expected.

In the West – and not only –
It resulted in a hothouse,
The last refuge
Of the once upon a time emperor.

The Iron Horse initially
And the "clones" of Ford subsequently
Brought about the sunset
Of the most valuable

Assistant of the descendants
Of Adam and Eve
In their climb
On the ladder of civilization.

Without Pegasus
Homo sapiens
Would still be

Examining the plans
For the improvement
Of the "palace" of Lascaux.

Truce for Katzura

It is the absolute delicacy
Of the gypsies.

The moment its smell
Hits their nostrils,
Be it from the charcoal or the stewpot,
The little gypsies run like the wind
To fetch a bite to their mother,

Carelessly pregnant
With their seventh brother.

They exchange hare-hounds
With bird ones

With Pointers
– specialists in the hunting of erinaceous –
Being their first choice.

They get both gratis…
Of course.

If in the country of the rising sun
The absence of fish on the table to the guest
Is reason for mutual hara-kiri

The presence of Katzura
On the plastic table of the tent
Is the ultimate honour to the guest.

His soft tooth for almonds
He paid occasionally
With his life.

Now if he isn't turned into fertiliser
By the blades of the milling-machine
In the olive-grove

Rarely will he manage
To cross the country road intact,

Let alone the municipal one.

The Russian roulette isn't but
A stroll around his burrow
By comparison.

A lot of brothers "depart"
Victims of the offshoots of Monsanto
Which permanently supplies

The farmers with weed-killers, pesticides
And all kinds of weapons
In the war they wage with Nature

His natural enemies
– with the exception of the fox –
Share the same annihilation.

The Almighty in his wisdom
Granted him hibernation,

A breath of jauntiness
In the permanent struggle
– for survival –
Without truce…

Falco peregrinus

Born breaker
Of the aerial speed-limit.

A wing-bearing missile
Of vertical assault
That brings instant death
To its flying target.

Scourge of rats.

A cosmopolitan hunter
With Antarctica being
The only intentionally neglected destination,
To his itinerary.

A true feminist
Proud of his girlfriend's
Superior size.

Food and security
Determine his residence
That varies from the Empire State Building
To the most decrepit of bridges.

Thanks to the few *Homo sapiens*
Friends of the species
He scraped through the DDT hell-period
Despite heavy losses.

This hunter by nature
Has nothing in common
With the "hawks" in green

Who have abducted
And abused his name
For decades now.

It is only to be expected therefore
That he bears the stain on his name
By the military warmongers
With the outmost aversion.

The Jumpers

Often in the winter, entirely by chance
And anywhere I come across some travellers.
With the first drops of rain
The frogs begin their Argonautic expedition.

Most of the time individually, sometimes however
In groups of three or four,
They try to cross
The road.

They are not in a hurry and give the impression
They have been born philosophers or thinkers.
They stop in the middle of the road
And enjoy the rain.

It doesn't seem to bother them
When they shall get over the danger.
The lights that blind them
Or the wheels next to them,

Sometimes even over some comrades,
Do not scare them in the least.
There on the road they insist
On offering their sacrifices to Athena.

How many of them will reach Colchis
Is unknown as indeed
If they are still interested
In the Golden Fleece.

A Prince

Omniscient
With two brains,

Compassionate
With three hearts,

Dandy,
Absolute sovereign
Of *haut-couture*,

He changes colour
Instantly
According to preference.

Par excellence gourmet,
His passage quite obvious,

Spread with *Carcinus*
And *Palinurus*.

Gentleman
Of geniality
And warm handshake.

A present of Poseidon
To the aristocracy
Of his domain.

The ambrosia
Of the liquid element.

In his search
The "Samurai"

Plough
The seas.

"Octopus vulgaris
Prince
of the Cephalopodi"

His card
Of introduction.

Sturnus vulgaris

Forget the *pas-de-deux*.

Here the Bolshoi, Kirov and The Royal Ballet
Are not orphaned
Of Nureyev and Fonteyn.

They simply do not need them,
They are superfluous.

With dance in their genes
This tribe
Exists to serve Terpsichore.

Harmony, speed and beauty
Rule here.

The individual does not exist,
He is unthinkable.

The whole
Consists of a huge *corps-de-ballet*.

It functions with one mind,
One soul,
One movement,

Performed by hundreds,
At times thousands
Of dance mystics.

Formations of incredible beauty
Are wiped out
From one moment to the next,

To be replaced
By even more beautiful, more delicate,
More complex choreographies.

In a ballet
Without Tchaikovsky, Prokofiev or Diaghilev
Not even an orchestra,

The suites of these ballerinas
Are executed
Without instruments,

As they climb, descend,
Move left, right,
Sideways,

They rush in all directions
Pretending a landing,

In order to shoot once again
With a steep left turn

To form
A perfect eight.

The intermission lasts seconds
And then in the air again.

Paraphrasing Descartes
"I dance therefore I exist"
The definition of their lives.

These polyglot
Fellow students of mynah
And parrot

With their libertine behaviour
And imperceptible gender

Are *bon-vivant*
With gourmet preferences
And an extended menu,

That is

Aristocrats
By definition.

A Family

"You talking to me?"
The absolute bully, *Speotyto cunicularia*,
Throws at your face.
As is well-known size doesn't matter
If you've got the bollocks
And this fellow
Not only possesses what it takes
But he also makes a song of it.

Another member,
The Benjamin of its kind,
Does not hesitate to enrich his menu
With scorpions
Despite the fact that he is
A born Casanova
Singing to the girls of his neighborhood
In order to attract the doll
That will mate with him.

Micrathene whitneyi is written
On his identity card, remember it.

And then the "Emperor"
Of the Far East walks on stage,
Not that he scorns Europe or Latin America,
Asio otus.
On hearing his name Asia comes to mind
Straightaway

And his countenance confirms your guess.
His ears – nothing of the kind –
Impose humility and respect.
His eyes disdain you entirely,
You can be wasting away for hours on end
In front of him without being rewarded
With a single glance.

These three wonderful fellows
Are members of the big family of *Ululae,*
Who amongst their other virtues
Count wisdom,

Since one of them
Has been and still remains
The trademark of the goddess
Patroness of the City of Athens.

Columba livia

The postman of the Romans
Sends his present-day *Homo sapiens* colleagues,
In spite of the aid of Google-Earth,
For further training.

Thanks to him Decius Brutus
Broke the siege of Mutina
Reducing to total uselessness
All the siege means of Marcus Antonius.

Top-notch marathon-runner of birds
With a steady long-drawn-out speed of over 150 kph
Leaves his arch-enemy, the champion of vertical diving
Falco peregrinus, in the superfluous basket.

Mr Reuters might not have succeeded to stand up
In the first steps of the founding of his news agency
Had it not been for the help of his 45 messengers.

The same can be said of Mr Rothschild
Who owes a considerable part of his empire
To the steady channel of communication of the family
That *Columba livia* safeguarded for him.

During WWI he was very often
The only contact of the front line
With the rear.

While in WWII he was,
According to the British Major General Fowler,
The *deus ex machina*, when every other means of communication
Was impossible.

His craving
For return to his dovecote
Turns him into a brother of Ulysses.

The gift of the Sumerians to mankind
Is the absolute courier
In all kinds of weather and terrain
And by definition an ecologist.

Lamentation

Theft is punished
Certainly, not by death,
If you are human,

If not
Things change.

His addiction
To his daily egg,
From the hencoop in the courtyard,
Cost the young crow
His life.

The spread of the news of his death
In the absence of witnesses is a mystery.

Parliament was convened instantly.
A lamentation as heart-breaking
As that of the Daughters of Troy
Began to vibrate the air,
By friends, acquaintances and total strangers.

With continuous circles and wailings
Over the body
The aerial rite
Lasted for hours.

The disappearance of the body
Did not improve the situation.

The next day
The same hour
On the exact spot,
Without the least decrease,
The wailing returned.

The rite was repeated
Daily
For a week.

The lamentation of the swarm
Put a definitive and irreversible end
To the hunting career
Of the executioner.

The A.S.O.

The nightly an after-hourly
      concert
An endless *largo sostenuto*.

Many colleagues of Beethoven,
If not the Maestro himself
Would reach the limits of despair
And perhaps tragedy

Confronted with such duration.

The rush of the swamp
Haunted aficionados
Among the musicians.

Tall, gigantic protectors, comrades
And at times musicians – wind willing.

The impeccable roof
Of the "musical palace"
– An ever-changing audience –

Pays tribute
To the Jihadists
Of phonetic music.

Exhausted at dawn
From the night-long performance

Soloists, first and second violins,
Violas, cellos, trombones

Begin to kneel to Morpheus.

The first rays encounter
The Amphibian Symphony Orchestra
In slumber.

For many members
The same nightmare
Returns,

On the table of one
Of the taverns
Of the city

The maestro and a number
Of brothers

Have been turned

Into appetizers.

Defendants

– The honourable defence may proceed to the tribune
But where are the defendants?

Monsieur Bartholomew Chassané cleared his
Throat twice and began his oration.

– I am absolutely certain that your honour shall
Be in full accord with me, given the dangers
My clients would be exposed to during their
Journey, bearing in mind the distance they would
Have had to cover in order to present themselves
Before the court – I am of course referring to
Their ancestral enemies, the cats, sworn, in
A manner of speaking, exterminators and hunters
Of the first order who demonstrate the utmost
Ability and invent countless methods in order to
Wipe out and devour the afore-named gentlemen –
Their arrival has not been
Possible, due to matters exclusively beyond their
Control and not in the slightest having to do
With any disrespect to the power of the court,
You so honourably serve.

This is how the rats scraped through sound and dry.

The same line of defence could not serve
As a precedent to the swine who – at the end
Of the fourteenth century in Normandy – disfigured
A child and was sentenced to garroting.

Bearing in mind that the execution of the sentence
Would be attended by the Viscount Falaise, the
Swine was dressed as befitted an aristocrat,
In waistcoat and gloves.

In the courts of Medieval Europe marched and
Was sentenced or acquitted an entire army of
Defendants – locusts, flies, birds, snails, worms,
Bulls, roosters, donkeys, goats, swine, etc.

The arms of the law did not escape even statues
Though they may have been those of the
Virgin herself.
In 946 in a small village in Wales one of her
Statues fell off its pedestal and killed a woman.

It was arrested and sentenced to death.
The villagers – for the sake of the Virgin –
Did not hang it but deserted it on the banks
Of the river; the tide moved it elsewhere.
The next day it was found "drowned and dead".

Up to the end of the 18th century the
Villagers carried the nickname "Jews of Hawarden".

And we may have fun with Antiquity and the
Middle Ages that sentenced objects and animals,
However, it is not at all improbable that tomorrow
We shall not be laughed at ourselves.

For our treatment of fellow human-beings
Who can resist crime as much as a bear can
Turn a blind eye to honey.

It took us some centuries in order to realise
That homosexuality is not an illness; let us
Hope that it shall take less in order to
Comprehend that the sentence on Pasaris

Does not differ much from those on the animals.

The Forest of the Rising Sun

The big sister of the city
Devours the little buzz entirely.

This worksite is inaudible
To the naked ear.

An invisible Charlie Chaplin
"Co-ordinates" the traffic.
The result is known.

With a load three times his size
Between his pincers
The blondish-red weight-lifter leads
The right column of porters;
The left one is returning to be loaded again.

Some time now a swarm of "Apaches",
Yellow with black stripes,
Is endeavouring to suck the nectar of the hydrangea.

Some plump young ladies,
With black spots on their magnificent
Red dresses, walk leisurely on the green carpet philosophising.

The students of the seminary
That has solidly partaken in the outing
Run pitch-black and unbridled in all directions.

Unmoved by the uproar a yellow-green longish lady
– Her Gucci glasses on the side –
Is sun-bathing in exultation.
A lot more groups colourful and different,
Architects, lumberjacks, miners, etc.
On the ground.

The aerial traffic competes with that of Narita.

In the two-bedroom flat of Yuko Yoshida
– 6th floor –
This wood of two square metres
Is bursting with life... in the heart of Tokyo
A bonsai... rainforest.

Orphaned of the spirits of the forest... though.

Swifts

With legs being
More of an invisible ornament
Rather than a necessity,

Swifts are true
To their family name
Apodidae (without legs).

They put *Columba livia* to shame
As the Hyper-Marathon-Runners
Par excellence,

With a yearly mileage
Equivalent to
Five girdles round the Earth.

Swaying a little
Sleeping is done in the air
As indeed is feeding.

A scourge for tiny insects,
Things get out of control
When feeding their chicks,

With a hundred thousand of them
Being
The daily ration.

A symbol of restlessness
And pursuit
In coats of arms

It depicted
The fourth son,
Free to seek his fortune.

With pesticides drastically reducing
Their food supply
And roof tiles, barns and old houses
A vanishing nursery amenity

The absolute emperor of the skies,

With hardly a landing a year,

Is entering the endangered species zone.

A most miserable prospect

For the Hercules of flying.

Dina

She wiped out a whole family in five nights.
Minutely following the hierarchy,

First the male, successively the mother
And last the offspring.

A lifetime on their guard the mice –
They do not dispose the luxury of absolute abandon

Of the domesticated or at least of some of them –
But in this case to no avail.

She has forgotten how many births she has sowed
And completely ignores with how many batches

She has provided the neighbourhood.
Indeed some of them are on duty

As frontier-guards on some of the most distant hencoops of the
    village.
The weasels of the area – victims *par excellence* –

Are still in the process of inventing
A plan to master the plague.

The flight of Tabi faced with her rage –
Absentmindedly he anchored in her territorial waters

For two minutes – dispatches the myth
Of the dog and the cat for revision.
And yes Dina shall come to an end of
Lannate, traffic-accident or rifle-shot but at least

Here where she was born. The other Dina,
The elder one, shall leave her bones

In Chicago in -40°C. With three children
There and none here in your 85th year,

If you are a human being and not a cat,
Others decide for you.

"I'll be damned if she hasn't got
The Colocotrony in her pocket metal-detectors or not"

Thought the younger Dina, leisurely "baking"
Herself on the wall of the deserted house like a dog.

Dog on Chain

For three days now
I can hardly move.
My legs exist only
To give the impression that I am sound in limb.

I stagger without
Having had a drop of alcohol.

More of a she-rabbit than a bitch
My mother produced us in batches.

I had a very narrow escape
And I was not drowned
Along with the rest of my brothers and sisters.

– Leave this one out, don't put it in the bag
I shall keep it to guard my hens.

Said Marigo
And grabbed me by the scruff of my neck.

While I was still young
I ran free like a little vagabond.

– He grew up, he will run away,
Tie him down.
She ordered her son, one morning.

One metre of rope and two of chain,
An iron bar in the ground
And my orbit was irrevocably determined.

My all-weather home
A Texaco barrel.

Barking would be of some use
When the foxes were not hungry,

Otherwise they would attack
The hencoop and depart loaded.

The next day
Marigo would beat me up.
She had to let off on somebody,
As she used to say.

My "escapes" were few and far between.
The choice was either
A slave with a full belly and safe
Or a vagabond, hungry and in danger
With the smell of powder in the nostrils.

I cannot remember how many I have sown
And I never had to find out.

I have heard that some of us
Are born with a silver spoon.

Without fleas, jiggers, crusts of bread,
Curses, kicks, rifles, poison-balls.
With veterinarians, medicine, clinics.

It is months now that
I am going from bad to worse
With terrible pains in my belly.

I have given up eating and I feel dizzy.
The jiggers have dried me out
And at night I hear my mother calling.

I see her now inviting me next to her.

– What shall we do with Dias?
Bury him or throw him on the dumping ground?

GLOSSARY

Asio otus   Long-eared owl

Carcinus   Type of crab

Colocotrony   Penknife, bearing the name of a Greek War
                       of Independence hero

Columba livia   Common pigeon ('rock dove')

Falco peregrinus   Peregrine falcon

Katzura   Roma word for hedgehog

Lannate   Deadly pesticide, often used to kill animals

Micrathene whitneyi   Elf owl

Octopus vulgaris   Common octopus

Palinurus   Type of spiny lobster

Pasaris   Greek Serial Killer

Speotyto cunicularia   Burrowing owl

Sturnus vulgaris   Common starling

Voucephalas   The horse of Alexander the Great; sometimes
                       spelt 'Bucephalus'

CPSIA information can be obtained
at www.ICGtesting.com
Printed in the USA
LVHW080658081221
705433LV00030B/1420